CATS

A BOOK OF DAYS

CATS

A BOOK OF DAYS

RHODA NOTTRIDGE

CRESCENT BOOKS
NEW YORK • AVENEL, NEW JERSEY

The Origin Of The Species

Welcome to the wonderful world of cats. Adored by the Egyptians, the cat enjoyed a long spell of exultation as one of their sacred beings. Also famed as pest control experts, enterprising cats happily hitched rides around the world aboard a plethora of sailing vessels, earning their keep guarding grain against the unwanted attentions of rats and mice. Every now and then, a curious cat would jump ship and settle somewhere, many miles from its home, in an exciting new port. It was easy enough to be accepted and soon they found humans here and there who they could adopt and train in the gentle art of cat care. The history of the cat has not always been a happy tail, for in the Middle Ages, poor puss with its beautiful eyes and psychic powers was horribly persecuted by witch hunters,

who believed it to be an accessory to evil. It took the cat a while to clear its name again. When we admire a complacent cat lying contentedly sprawled out on our laps, we should perhaps be grateful that our feline friends do not dwell on their treatment by humans in those past times. Fortunately for the feline, cats have been celebrated again for the last few centuries as creatures of great elegance. Apart from the ancestors of the sailing ships' cats, unusual and exotic cats of all kinds can now be found around the world, many the ancestors of cats bought, sold or bargained for by travellers over the years. The Cat Lovers' Birthday Book purrs with the celebration of cats both fickle and famous. And as you note down the birthdays of your friends and relations, you will see whether they share their day with other, more celebrated members of the cat fancy. You will also be able to observe what is written in the stars about cats – and their owners...

A cosy family
LEON HUBER

JANUARY

The Ancient Cat

OUR DEVOTION TO CATS goes back at least 3,000 years, to ancient Egyptian times. To the Egyptians, cats were absolutely sacred and the cat cult was so strong that felines remained in great favour for around 2,000 years. A whole city was given over to cats, who had a temple devoted to their worship and a cat-goddess who oversaw all felines. The Sun God, Ra, was said to turn into a cat every morning at dawn. By so doing, he drove away Apep, the serpent of darkness, for another day. The death of a household cat was reverently mourned and the cat often mummified before burial in one of the huge cat cemeteries, which contained the bodies of thousands of cats now purring peacefully in an after-life. The family who lived with the cat would shave off their eyebrows as a mark of mourning.

A birthday surprise of BURMESE kittens

*January cats
snuggle in warm
winter fur and hold the
promise of summer
sunshine deep in their
amber eyes.*

GLOWING EMBERS

The Egyptians believed that cats absorbed the fire of the sun through their eyes. At night, the sun was reflected in cats' eyes, and so long as their eyes glowed, the sun would rise again the next day.

SAT   1

SUN   2

MON   3

TUES ~~4~~

WED   5

THURSDAY   6

FRIDAY   7

NOTES

JANUARY

8

9

10

11

12

WES
JOYCE   10:15 A M. 9 JULIE

13

14

NOTES

MILK FOR THE CAT

When the tea is brought at five o'clock,
   And all the neat curtains are drawn with care,
The little black cat with bright green eyes
   Is suddenly purring there.

At first she pretends, having nothing to do,
   She has come in merely to blink by the grate,
But though tea may be late or the milk may be sour,
   She is never late.

And presently her agate eyes
   Take a soft large milky haze,
And her independent casual glance
   Becomes a stiff, hard gaze.

Then she stamps her claws or lifts her ears
   Or twists her tail and begins to stir,
Till suddenly all her little body becomes
   One breathing, trembling purr.

*I am as
vigilant as a cat to
steal cream.*
WILLIAM
SHAKESPEARE

The children eat and wriggle and laugh;
  The two old ladies stroke their silk:
But the cat is grown small and thin with desire,
  Transformed to a creeping lust for milk.

The white saucer like some full moon descends
  At last from the cloud of the table above;
She sighs and dreams and thrills and glows,
  Transfigured with love.

She nestles over the shining rim,
  Buries her chin in the creamy sea;
Her tail hangs loose; each drowsy paw
  Is doubled under each bending knee.

A long dim ecstasy holds her life;
  Her world is an infinite shapeless white,
Till her tongue has curled the last holy drop;
  Then she sinks back into the night,

Draws and dips her body to heap
  Her sleepy nerves in the great arm-chair,
Lies defeated and buried deep
  Three or four hours unconscious there.

HAROLD MUNRO *(1879–1932)*

Kittens celebrate with a dish of creamy milk.

A BIRTHDAY TREAT

Always reserve a generous slice of your
cream-stuffed birthday cake for puss
– she will only steal it for herself if you don't.

FUR AT THE FIRESIDE

A blazing fire, a warm rug, candles lit and curtains drawn, the kettle on for tea, and finally, the cat before you, attracting your attention - it is a scene that everybody likes. The cat purrs, as if it applauded your consideration, and gently moves its tail. What an odd expression of the power to be irritable and the will to be pleased there is in its face, as it looks up at us!

Now she proceeds to clean herself all over, having a just sense of the demands of her elegant person, beginning judiciously with her paws, and fetching amazing tongues at her hind-hips. Anon, she scratches her neck with a foot of rapid delight, leaning her head towards it, and shutting her eyes half to accommodate the action of the skin, and half to enjoy the luxury. She then rewards her paws with a few more touches - look at the action of her head and neck, how pleasing it is, the ears pointed forward, and the neck gently arching to and fro. Finally, she gives a sneeze, and another twist of mouth and whiskers, and then, curling her tail towards her front claws, settles herself on her hind quarters in an attitude of bland meditation.

What does she think of? - of her saucer of milk at breakfast? or of the thump she got yesterday in the kitchen for stealing the meat? or of her own meat, the Tartar's dish, noble horse-flesh? or of her friend the cat next door, the most impassioned of serenaders? or of her little ones, some of whom are now large, and all of them gone? Is that among her recollections when she looks pensive? Does she taste of the noble prerogative sorrows of man?

LEIGH HUNT (1784–1859)

Beautiful present sufficingness of a cat's imagination!
Confined to the snug circle of her own sides,
and the two next inches of rug or carpet.
LEIGH HUNT

15

16

17

18

19

20

21

NOTES

CAPRICORNIANS (DECEMBER 23 – JANUARY 19)
Admirers of hierarchy and discipline, ritual and routine, they are enlivened by a generous dash of flirtatious caprice. They applaud the self-contained independence of cats and appreciate the connection with the royal house of Egypt; they also delight in the cat's streak of playfulness in the midst of dignity. Capricorns like status, and so may choose a prestigious pedigree to share their well-ordered home.

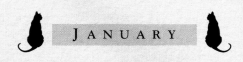

WHAT'S IN A NAME?

The naming of a cat or kitten is no simple matter. Cats can be honoured with the most classical of titles but will often refuse to answer to a name they think unsuitable for themselves.

The philosopher Jeremy Bentham was a man more at ease with a cat for company and he conferred an increasing number of titles on his friend. The cat began life as Langbourne, and as he matured, he was knighted by Bentham to become Sir John Langbourne. As Sir John, the cat was rather a keen seducer of frisky females of his species around the garden. As the cat reached later life, he became a calmer and increasingly pensive puss, showing more of an interest in the metaphysical elements of life. So he was granted a doctorate in divinity by Bentham. His title, finally, was The Reverend Sir John Langbourne, D.D.

FELIX, *the best-known name for cats, comes from the Latin word for lucky. There are 66 saints named Felix.*

22

23

24

25

26

27

Lewis Carroll born, 1832

28

NOTES

29

30

31

NOTES

Capricorn cats are polite and formal,
climb high and consort with kings.

THE NAMING OF KITTENS

Our old cat has kittens three -
What do you think their names should be?

One is tabby with emerald eyes,
And a tail that's long and slender,
And into a temper she quickly flies
If you ever by chance offend her.
I think we shall call her this -
I think we shall call her that -
Now, don't you think that Pepperpot
Is a nice name for a cat?

One is black with a frill of white,
And her feet are all white fur,
If you stroke her she carries her
  tail upright
And quickly begins to purr.
I think we shall call her this -
I think we shall call her that -
Now, don't you think that Sootikin
Is a nice name for a cat?

One is tortoiseshell yellow and black,
With plenty of white about him;
If you tease him, at once he sets up his back,
He's a quarrelsome one, ne'er doubt him.
I think we shall call him this -
I think we shall call him that -
Now, don't you think that Scratchaway
Is a nice name for a cat?

THOMAS HOOD *(1799–1845)*

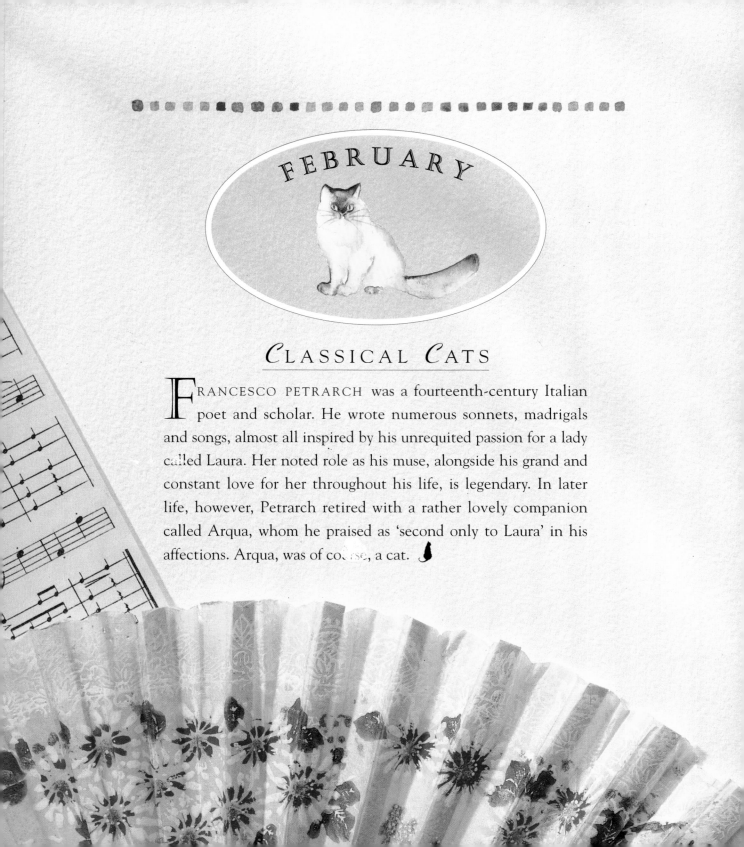

FEBRUARY

CLASSICAL CATS

FRANCESCO PETRARCH was a fourteenth-century Italian poet and scholar. He wrote numerous sonnets, madrigals and songs, almost all inspired by his unrequited passion for a lady called Laura. Her noted role as his muse, alongside his grand and constant love for her throughout his life, is legendary. In later life, however, Petrarch retired with a rather lovely companion called Arqua, whom he praised as 'second only to Laura' in his affections. Arqua, was of course, a cat.

PETRARCH'S PUSS

The Tuscan bard of deathless fame
Nursed in his breast a double flame,
Unequally divided;
And when I say I had his heart,
While Laura played the second part,
I must not be derided.

For my fidelity was such,
It merited regard as much
As Laura's grace and beauty;
She first inspired the poet's lay,
But since I drove the mice away,
His love repaid my duty.

Through all my exemplary life,
So well did I in constant strife
Employ my claws and curses,
That even now though I am dead,
Those nibbling wretches dare not tread
On one of Petrarch's verses.

TRANSLATED FROM THE LATIN BY
ANTONIUS QUAERINGUS

ROMAN REMAINS

Since classical times, cats have run riot in the city of
Rome. An innocent feline stalking around the
Forum today may well have a past to be proud of; legend
has it that the souls of wicked Roman Emperors return to
their former pleasure palaces in feline form.

*February cats roam
wild and free.*

1

2

3

4

5

6

7
Charles Dickens born, 1812

NOTES

In February, cats go to Rome.
FRENCH PROVERB

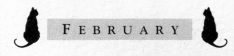

Willow contemplates the universe;
the Aquarian feline is the original curious cat.

FIRM FRIENDS

Cats seem capable of surpassing their instincts from time to time, to make friends with animals that are normally their adversaries, and to adopt them as play pals. From dogs to ducks, they overcome their ordinary appetites for the sake of a special friend. In this case, a rather large acquaintance . . .

TRUNKS AND TAILS

In the great Zoological Gardens . . . the boon companion of the colossal elephant was a common cat! This cat had a fashion of climbing up the elephant's hind legs, and roosting on his back. She would sit up there, with her paws curved under her breast, and sleep in the sun half the afternoon. It used to annoy the elephant at first and he would reach up and take her down, but she would go aft and climb up again. She persisted until she finally conquered the elephant's prejudices, and now they are inseparable friends. The cat plays about her comrade's forefeet or his trunk often, until dogs approach, and then she goes aloft out of danger. The elephant has annihilated several dogs lately, that pressed his companion too closely.

MARK TWAIN (1835–1919)

FEBRUARY

8

9

10

11

12
Feast Day of St Felix

13

14

NOTES

The President's splendid whiskers demonstrate
the dandy in the Aquarian cat's soul.

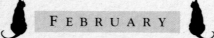

THE CAT AND THE COCKROACH

15

Jeremy Bentham born, 1748

16

17

18

19

20

21

NOTES

*M*ehitabel was an alley cat, immortalised in the verse opposite by a literary cockroach called Archy, who secretly types out his poems by jumping around on an old office typewriter.

Orlando pines for the faithless Mehitabel

Mehitabel of the umpteen lives is a typical Aquarian cat – free-living and free-loving, eccentric, footloose and fancy free. Her name is Hebrew for God makes Happy.

THE SONG OF MEHITABEL

*t*his is the song of mehitabel
of mehitabel the alley cat
as i wrote you before boss
mehitabel is a believer
in the pythagorean
theory of the transmigration
of the souls and she claims
that formerly her spirit
was incarnated in the body
of cleopatra
that was a long time ago
and one must not be
surprised if mehitabel
has forgotten some of her
more regal habits

i have had my ups and downs
but wotthehell wotthehell
yesterday sceptres and crowns
fried oysters and velvet gowns
and today i herd with bums
but wotthehell wotthehell

i wake the world from sleep
as i caper and sing and leap
when i sing my wild free tune
wotthehell wotthehell
under the blear eyed moon
i am pelted with cast off shoon
but wotthehell wotthehell

i once was an innocent kit
wotthehell wotthehell
with a ribbon my neck to fit
and bells tied onto it
o wotthehell wotthehell
but a maltese cat came by
with a come hither look in his eye
and a song that soared to the sky
and wotthehell wotthehell
and i followed adown the street
the pad of his rhythmical feet
o permit me again to repeat
wotthehell wotthehell

my youth i shall never forget
but there s nothing i really regret
wotthehell wotthehell
there s a dance in the old dame yet
toujours gai toujour gai

the things that i had not ought to
i do because i ve gotto
wotthehell wotthehell
and i end with my favourite motto
toujours gai toujours gai

ARCHY
DON MARQUIS *(1878–1937)*

 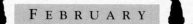

With his long bushy tail and fluffy ears,
Albert really looks in charge.

KING CATS

*W*ithout a doubt the cat considers itself the regal ruler of home and garden. Finding a suitable sentry post, such as on top of a wobbly wall, the cat will position itself in such a manner that it can observe from a dignified height what nonsense goes on below. From there it casts a disdainful eye on babbling passers-by, or mentally maps out elaborate extensions to its territories that have yet to be confirmed as within the bounds of reason in the eyes of its neighbouring feline friends.

CAT IN CHARGE

I am monarch of all I survey,
My right there is none to dispute;
From the centre all round to the sea
I am lord of the fowl and the brute.

WILLIAM COWPER *(1731–1800)*

*I'm the king of the castle
And you're the dirty rascal!*
TRADITIONAL NURSERY
RHYME

*'A cat may look at a king' was originally the
title of a seventeenth-century political pamphlet,
suggesting we are all equal.*

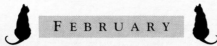

22

23

24

25

26

27

28/29

NOTES

AQUARIANS (JANUARY 20 - FEBRUARY 19)

Eccentric, unpredictable, clever and intuitive themselves, they find a soul mate in the cat. They truly appreciate the cat's mysterious otherness and consummate self-possession. A cat sharing an Aquarian's open-plan living space will often belong to an unusual breed – Manx say, or Scottish Fold, or Cornish Rex.

MARCH

CHURCH CATS

DURING THE SIXTEENTH and seventeenth centuries, when many a poor puss was persecuted, Cardinal Richelieu kept a room in his palace devoted to his cats, where two servants fed the creatures the best *foie gras* France could offer. Pope Pius IX and Leo XII all hand-fed their favourite Vatican cats. Leo XII may well have been the pope who gave audiences with a cat secreted on his lap. Presumably the cat was not as well concealed within the robes as the pope supposed, for the story to be still told today. A dangling paw or suspiciously furry tail poking out from under the religious robes may well have given the game away. One deeply religious cat appears to have belonged in the sixteenth century to the English Cardinal Thomas Wolsey. The cat was said always to attend mass if the cardinal was celebrating it.

Piscean cats, like many Piscean people, are attracted to religious cults. Devout cats have been kept by many saints, including the sixteenth century saint Philip Neri.

THE MONK & HIS CAT PANGUR

I and my white Pangur
Have each his special art:
His mind is set on hunting mice,
Mine is upon my special craft.

I love to rest - better than any fame! -
With close study at my little book;
White Pangur does not envy me:
He loves his childish play.

When in our house we two are all alone -
A tale without tedium.
We have - sport never-ending!
Something to exercise our wit.

At times by feats of derring-do
A mouse sticks in his net,
While into my net there drops
A difficult problem of hard meaning.

He points his full shining eye
Against the fence of the wall:
I point my clear though feeble eye
Against the keenness of science.

He rejoices with quick leaps
When in his sharp claw sticks a mouse;
I, too, rejoice when I have grasped
A problem difficult and dearly loved.

Though we are thus at all time,
Neither hinders the other,
Each of us pleased with his own art
Amuses himself alone.

He is master of the work
Which every day he does:
While I am at my own work
To bring difficulty to clearness.

8TH CENTURY IRISH MONK

1

2

3

4

5

6

7
Feast Day of St Felicity

NOTES

 MARCH

A VERY FINE CAT INDEED

The famous English writer, critic and lexicographer, Dr Samuel Johnson, was fond of felines. His biographer James Boswell was less enchanted by them but was forced to tolerate Johnson's pampered pet in order to spend time with the great man. Boswell was particularly bothered by the spoilt Hodge. . .

HODGE

I never shall forget the indulgence with which he treated Hodge, his cat; for whom he himself used to go out and buy oysters, lest the servants having that trouble should take a dislike to the poor creature. . .
I recollect him one day scrambling up Dr Johnson's breast, apparently with much satisfaction, while my friend, smiling and half-whistling, rubbed down his back, and pulled him by the tail and when I observed he was a fine cat, saying, 'Why, yes, Sir, but I have had cats whom I liked better than this'; and then, as if perceiving Hodge to be out of countenance, adding, 'but he is a very fine cat, a very fine cat indeed.'

THE LIFE OF SAMUEL JOHNSON

8

9

10

11

12

13

14

NOTES

This reminds me of the ludicrous account which he gave Mr Langton of the despicable state of a young gentleman of good family -'Sir, when I heard of him last, he was running about town, shooting cats.' And then, in a sort of kindly reverie, he bethought himself of his own favourite cat, and said, 'But Hodge shan't be shot: no, no Hodge shall not be shot.'

THE LIFE OF SAMUEL JOHNSON
JAMES BOSWELL (1740–1795)

PISCEANS (FEBRUARY 20 – MARCH 20)
Sensitive, emotional and intuitive themselves, they appreciate the cat's effortless empathy with human distress and worry. All cats know that Pisceans are a pushover as owners; they are the sign of the fish, after all.

A typical
Piscean cat, *Fiddlesticks* oozes
charm and sympathy.

CRUEL CATTES

*O*n all the whole nacyon
Of cattes wylde and tame;
God send them sorrow and shame!
That cat especyally
That slew so cruelly
My lytell pretty sparowe.

JOHN SKELTON *(1460–1529)*

LITTLE ROBIN REDBREAST

*L*ittle Robin Redbreast sat upon a tree,
Up went the Pussy-cat, and down went he,
Down came Pussy-cat, away Robin ran;
Says little Robin Redbreast: 'Catch me if you can!'

Little Robin Redbreast jumped upon a spade,
Pussy-cat jumped after him, and then he was afraid.
Little Robin chirped and sang, and what did Pussy say?
Pussy-cat said: 'Mew, mew, mew,' and Robin flew away.

MOTHER GOOSE *(C.1760)*

15

16

17

18

19

20

21

NOTES

SORROW AND SHAME

*E*very cat owner knows the mixed emotion of their favourite feline proudly catching their first bird. Alexander Dumas had a cat called Mysouff II, which ate Dumas' entire exotic bird collection. Dumas called a trial which the cat was obliged to attend the following Sunday, during a dinner party. The guests were presented with the feathery facts. That the aviary door had been left open was brought up in Musouff II's defence but nonetheless, the poor puss was sentenced by the guests to a hefty five years' imprisonment in the monkeys' cage. Fortunately for Mysouff, Dumas suffered financial hardship shortly after the trial and the monkeys were sold and Mysouff was released from captivity.

Cruel, but composed and bland,
Dumb, inscrutable and grand,
So Tiberius might have sat
Had Tiberius been a cat.
MATTHEW ARNOLD

22

23

24

25

26

27

28

NOTES

THE COLLEGE CAT

*W*ithin those halls where student zeal
Hangs every morn on learning's lips,
Intent to make its daily meal
Of tips,

While drones the conscientious Don
Of Latin Prose, of Human Will,
Of Aristotle and of John
Stuart Mill,

We mouth with stern didactic air:
We prate of this, we rant of that:
While slumbers on his favourite chair
The Cat!

For what is Mill, and what is Prose,
Compared with warmth, and sleep, and food,
- All which collectively compose
The Good?

Although thy unreceptive pose
In presence of eternal Truth
No virtuous example shows
To youth,

Sleep on, O Cat! serenely through
My hurricanes of hoarded lore,
Nor seek with agitated mew
The door:

Thy calm repose I would not mar,
Nor chase thee forth in angry flight
Protesting loud (though some there are
Who might),

Because to my reflective mind
Thou dost from generations gone
Recall a wholly different kind
Of Don,

Who took his glass, his social cup,
And having quaffed it, mostly sat
Curled (metaphorically) up
Like that!

Far from those scenes of daily strife
And seldom necessary fuss
Wherein consists the most of life
For us,

When movements moved, they let them move:
When problems raged, they let them rage:
And quite ignored the Spirit of
The Age.

Of such thou wert the proper mate,
O peaceful-minded quadruped!
But liv'st with fellows up to date
Instead -

With men who spend their vital span
In petty stress and futile storm,
And for a recreation plan
Reform:

Whom pupils ne'er in quiet leave,
But throng their rooms in countless hordes:
Who sit from morn to dewy eve
On Boards:

Who skim but erudition's cream,
And con by night and cram by day
Such subjects as the likeliest seem
To pay!

But thou, from cares like these exempt,
Our follies dost serenely scan,
Professing thus thy just contempt
For Man:

For well thou knowest, that wished-for goal
Which still to win we vainly pine,
That calm tranquillity of soul
Is thine!

ALFRED GODLEY (1856–1925)

Winston

29

30

31

NOTES

*Piscean cats are pulled two ways;
they can switch from a cuddly comforter to a ruthless
killing machine in a twitch of their well-groomed tails.*

APRIL

Magic And The Moon

THE CAT HAS LONG BEEN LINKED with magic and mysteries. In Britain, a black cat entering a house is said to bring in good luck. In North America, white cats bring good fortune. Black cats are thought by some to be ruled by the moon, the pupils of their eyes noticeably expanding and contracting with the waxing and waning of the moon.

Kiss the black cat, An' 'twill make ye fat;
Kiss the white ane, 'twill make ye lean.
ENGLISH FOLKLORE

1

2

MONDAY **3**

10:00AM DEN + I DENTIST

4

Algernon Swinburne born, 1837

5

6

7

NOTES

THE CAT AND THE MOON

The cat went here and there
   And the moon spun round like a top
And the nearest kin of the moon,
   The creeping cat, looked up.
Black Minnaloushe stared at the moon,
   For, wander and wail as he would,
The pure cold light in the sky
   Troubled his animal blood.
Minnaloushe runs in the grass
   Lifting his delicate feet.
Do you dance, Minnaloushe, do you dance?
   When two close kindred meet,
What better than call a dance?
   Maybe the moon may learn,
Tired of that courtly fashion
   A new dance turn.
Minnaloushe creeps through the grass
   From moonlit place to place,
The sacred moon overhead
   Has taken a new phase.
Does Minnaloushe know that his pupils
   Will pass from change to change,
And that from round to crescent,
   From crescent to round they range?
Minnaloushe creeps through the grass
   Alone, important and wise,
And lifts to the changing moon
   His changing eyes.

WILLIAM BUTLER YEATS (1865–1939)

*April cats dance and
play in the rain.*

CUNNING KITTEN

A very hungry fox was prowling one moonlit night about a farmhouse, and he met a little kitten.

'You're not much of a meal for a starving creature,' he said. 'But in these hard times something is always better than nothing.'

'Oh, don't eat me!' said the kitten. 'I know where the farmer keeps his cheeses. Come with me and see.'

She led him into the farmyard, where there was a deep well with two buckets.

'Now, look in here, and you will see these cheeses.' she said.

8

9
Charles Baudelaire born, 1821

10

11
Christopher Smart born, 1722

12

13

14

NOTES

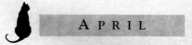

The fox peered down the well, and saw the moon reflected in the water.

'This is the way down,' said the kitten, jumping into the top bucket. Round and round rattled the rope-wheel, and down went the kitten into the water. Happily, she had gone down before, and she knew what to do, and climbing out of the bucket, she clung on to the rope.

'Can't you bring up one of these cheeses?' said the fox.

'No; they are too heavy,' said the kitten. 'You must come down.'

Now, the two buckets were connected, so that when one went down the other came up. As the fox was much heavier than his little companion his bucket went down and the water drowned him, while the kitten came up laughing and escaped.

AESOP'S FABLES

The highest climbing kitten on record was a four month-old which followed a group of climbers up to the peak of the Matterhorn in the Swiss Alps, notching up 4478 metres.

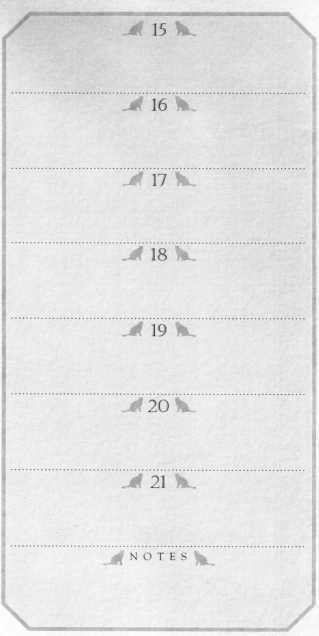

15

16

17

18

19

20

21

NOTES

MEUZZA AND MOHAMMED

This beautiful rug is the favourite place of
Cinnabar, a TABBY-POINT SIAMESE.

The Islamic prophet Mohammed lived from around 570 - 632 AD. He had a favourite cat called Meuzza. One day the prophet was called to prayer, but Meuzza was still soundly asleep on the sleeve of Mohammed's robe. Instead of disturbing his favourite cat, Mohammed cut off the sleeve of the robe to let the cat continue its slumbers.

Later Mohammed returned from his prayers and when Meuzza awoke, he arched his back to show his gratitude. Mohammed stroked the cat three times, which granted Meuzza a place forever in the Islamic Paradise. This also gave all cats in the world the ability always to land on their paws, protecting them forever from the danger of falling awkwardly after a precarious jump.

The cat's dreams are all about mice.
ARAB PROVERB

ARIENS (MARCH 21 – APRIL 20)
Bold, intrepid, adventurous risk takers themselves, they admire the cat's enterprise agility and independence. Only cats who can look after themselves should consort with an Arien, who will be far too busy running the world to bother with regular feeding times.

22

23

24

25

26

27

28

NOTES

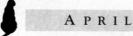

TIGER LEAPS AND FIRST FALLS

That way look, my Infant, lo!
What a pretty baby-show!
See the Kitten on the wall,
Sporting with the leaves that fall,
Withered leaves - one - two -
    and three -
From the lofty elder-tree!
Through the calm and
    frosty air
Of this morning
    bright and fair,
Eddying round and
    round they sink
Softly, slowly: one might
    think,
From the motions that are made,
Every little leaf conveyed
Sylph or Faery hither tending, -
To this lower world descending,
Each invisible and mute,
In his wavering parachute.

- But the Kitten, how she starts,
Crouches, stretches, paws, and darts!
First at one, and then its fellow,
Just as light and just as yellow;
There are many now - now one -
Now they stop and there are none:
What intenseness of desire
In her upward eye of fire!
With a tiger-leap half-way
Now she meets the coming prey,
Lets it go as fast, and then
Has it in her power again:
Now she works with three or four
Like an Indian conjuror;
Quick as he in feats of art,
Far beyond in joy of heart.
Were her antics played in the eye
Of a thousand standers-by,
Clapping hands with shout and stare,
What would little Tabby care
For the plaudits of the crowd?
Over happy to be proud,
Over wealthy in the treasure
Of her own exceeding pleasure!

THE KITTEN AND FALLING LEAVES
WILLIAM WORDSWORTH
(1770–1850)

Little *Catkins* sets forth,
a fearless and adventurous April-born kitten.

*Do you see that kitten
chasing so prettily her own tail?
If you could look with eyes, you
might see her surrounded with
hundreds of figures performing
complex dramas, with tragic and
comic issues, long conversations,
many characters, many ups
and downs of fate.*
R. W. EMERSON

29

30

NOTES

MAY

The Nature Of The Beast

CATS ARE OF DIVERS COLOURS; but for the most part gryseld like to congealed yse, which commeth from the condition of her meate; her head is like unto the head of a Lyon, except in her sharpe eares: her flesh is soft and smooth: her eies glister above measure especially when a man commeth to see a cat on the sudden, and in the night they can hardly be endured for their flaming aspect. ♪ It is a neate and cleanely creature, oftentimes licking hir own body to keepe it smooth and faire, having naturally a flexible backe for this purpose, and washing hir face with hir fore feet, but some observe that if she put her feete beyond the crowne of her head, that it is a presage of raine, and if the backe of a cat be thinne, the beast is of no courage or value. ♪

*I*t is needeless to spend any time about her loving nature to man, how she flattereth by rubbing her skinned against ones Legges, how she whurleth with her voyce, having as many tunes as turnes, for she hath one voyce to beg and to complain, another to testifie her delight and pleasure, another among hir own kind by flattring, by hissing, by purring, by spitting, insomuch as some have thought that they have a peculiar intelligible language among themselves.

Therefore, how she beggeth, playeth, leapeth, looketh, catcheth, tosseth with her foote, riseth up to strings held over her head, sometime creeping, sometime on the bely, snatching, now with mouth, and anon with foote, apprehending greedily any thing save the hand of a man, with divers such gestical actions, it is needeless to stand upon: insomuch as Coelius was wont to say that being free from his Studies and more urgent waighty affaires, he was not ashamed to play and sport himselfe with a Cat.

THE HISTORIE OF FOURE-FOOTED BEASTES, *1607*
EDWARD TOPSELL, NATURALIST

What astonished him was that cats should have two holes cut in their coats exactly at the places where their eyes were.
G.C. LICHTENBERG

1

2

3

4

5

6

7

NOTES

Kittens born in May are bound to be badly behaved.
CELTIC BELIEF

TABBIES AND TORTOISESHELLS

The tabby cat is the most common type of domestic cat. Back in Elizabethan England, a new, blotchy kind of cat began to appear, a trifle less tigerish in appearance compared to the striped cats known as mackerel tabbies. This tabby became ubiquitous around the globe as a favourite kind of ship's cat, which like the sailors, had a female friend in every port.

8

9

10

11
Edward Lear born, 1812

12

13

14

NOTES

THREE TABBIES

Three tabbies took out their cats to tea,
As well-behaved tabbies as well could be:
Each sat in the chair that each preferred,
They mewed for their milk, and they sipped
  and purred.
Now tell me this (as these cats you've seen them)
How many lives had these cats between them?

KATE GREENAWAY (1846–1901)

SLIM ODDS

The chances of finding a male tortoiseshell cat
are two hundred to one. They are highly prized
by Japanese fisherman as they are said to
protect sailors at sea and keep away
mischievous ghosts.

TAUREANS (APRIL 21 – MAY 21)
Handsome, cultured and pleasure-
loving, they respond to the cat's sleek
beauty and huge talent for idle
hedonism. Cats sharing a Taurean's
quietly luxurious home will be
well-fed and well-groomed but
must behave beautifully in return
for their pampering.

THE TORTOISESHELL CAT

The tortoiseshell cat
  She sits on the mat,
As gay as a sunflower she;
  In orange and black you see her blink,
And her waistcoat's white, and her nose is pink,
  And her eyes are the green of the sea.
But all is vanity, all the way;
  Twilight comings and close of day,
And every cat in the twilight's gray,
  Every possible cat.

The tortoiseshell cat,
  She is smooth and fat,
And we call her Josephine,
  Because she weareth upon her back
This coat of colours, this raven black,
  This red of the tangerine;
But all is vanity, all the way;
  Twilight follows the brightest day,

And every cat in the twilight's gray,
  Every possible cat.

PUNCH

Rubbing warts against the tail of
a tortoiseshell tom during the
month of May will make them
disappear, according to an old
English tradition.

Sweet, sleek and round,
Jemima is a typical Taurean puss.

*As an inspiration to the
author, I do not think the cat
can be over-estimated.*
CARL VAN VECHTEN

15

16

17

18

19

20

21

NOTES

MAY

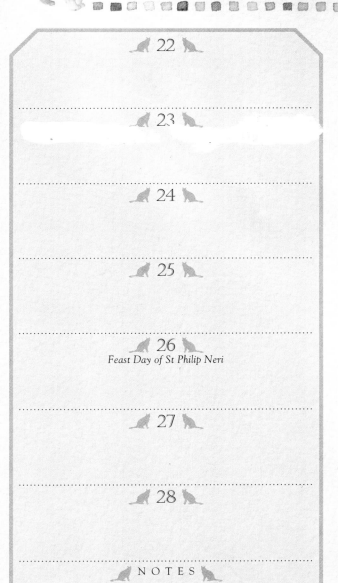

22

23

24

25

26
Feast Day of St Philip Neri

27

28

NOTES

LITERARY LITTERS

The author Charles Dickens enjoyed the attentions of cats, with a charming creature called William who was renamed Wilhelmina on the birth of a fine litter of kittens. Wilhelmina appeared to want a good education for her kittens, as she insisted on dragging them from their designated home in the kitchen with the servants and depositing them in the master's study at his feet.

One of these kittens was deaf and as nobody wanted it, he was kept and simply called the Master's Cat. In the evening, the cat, bored with watching Dickens sitting reading, learnt to distract the master's attention by extinguishing the candle with a swipe of its paw, making further work impossible and a few minutes of chin chucking essential.

DIVINE INSPIRATION

They come to sit on the table by the writer, keeping his thoughts company, and gazing at him with intelligent tenderness and magical penetration. It seems as though cats divine the thought that is passing from the brain to the pen, and that as they stretch out a paw, they are trying to seize it on its way.

MEMOIRS OF BAUDELAIRE
THEOPHILE GAUTIER (1811–1872)

PAWS AND PAPER

He loved books and when he found one open on the table he would lie down on it, turn over the edges of the leaves with his paw, and after a while, fall asleep, for all the world as if he had been reading a fashionable novel.

THÉOPHILE GAUTIER (1811–1872)

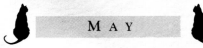

MAY

ODE ON THE DEATH OF A FAVOURITE CAT,
DROWNED IN A TUB OF GOLDFISHES

'Twas on a lofty vase's side
　Where China's gayest art had dyed
The azure flowers, that blow;
　Demurest of the tabby kind,
The pensive Selima, reclined,
　Gazed on the lake below.

Her conscious tail her joy declared;
　The fair round face, the snowy beard,
The velvet of her paws,
　Her coat, that with the tortoise vies,
Her ears of jet, and emerald eyes,
　She saw; and purr'd applause.

Still had she gazed; but 'midst the tide
　Two angel forms were seen to glide,
The genii of the stream:
　Their scaly armour's Tyrian hue
Through richest purple to the view
　Betray'd a golden gleam.

The hapless nymph with wonder saw:
　A whisker first, and then a claw,
With many an ardent wish,
　She stretch'd, in vain, to reach the prize
What female heart can gold despise?
　What cat's averse to fish?

Presumptuous maid! with looks intent
　Again she stretch'd, again she bent,
Nor knew the gulf between.
　(Malignant Fate sat by, and smiled)
The slipp'ry verge her feet beguiled,
　She tumbled headlong in.

29

30
Feast Day of Pope St Felix

31

*E*ight times emerging from the flood
 She mew'd to ev'ry wat'ry God,
Some speedy aid to send.
 No Dolphin came, no Nereid stirr'd:
No cruel Tom, nor Susan heard.
 A fav'rite has no friend!

From hence, ye beauties, undeceived,
 Know, one false step is ne'er retrieved,
And be with caution bold.
 Not all that tempts your wand'ring eyes
And heedless hearts is lawful prize.
 Not all that glitters, gold.

THOMAS GRAY *(1716–1771)*

*Poor Selima must have been a
Taurean cat, seduced by beauty and
the prospect of a gourmet dinner.*

✦ N O T E S ✦

*Taurean cats are smooth and handsome; they love
comfort, good food and music; theirs are the tuneful
caterwauls of the midnight concerts on the rooftops.*

*Fain would the
cat love fish to eat,
But she's loath
to wet her feet.*
TRADITIONAL

JUNE

A Moving Experience

THE VICTORIAN ARTIST and writer Edward Lear, famous for his nonsense rhymes, had a great penchant for a puss called Foss. When Lear had to move house to San Remo, he worried that it might upset Foss, so he insisted the architects design a house which was an absolute replica of his last one, apparently so that dear Foss might not be too unsettled by the move. Foss lived to the grand old age of seventeen, despite the move.

THE OWL AND THE PUSSY CAT

The Owl and the Pussy-cat went to sea
In a beautiful pea-green boat,
They took some honey, and plenty of money,
Wrapped up in a five-pound note.
The Owl looked up to the stars above,
And sang to a small guitar,
'O lovely Pussy! O Pussy, my love,
What a beautiful Pussy you are,
 You are,
 You are!
What a beautiful Pussy you are!'

Pussy said to Owl, 'You elegant fowl!
How charmingly sweet you sing!
O let us be married! too long we have tarried:
But what shall we do for a ring?
They sailed away, for a year and a day,
To the land where the Bong-tree grows
And there in a wood a piggy-wig stood
With a ring at the end of his nose,
 His nose,
 His nose,
With a ring at the end of his nose.

'Dear Pig, are you willing to sell for one shilling
Your ring?' Said the Piggy, 'I will.'
So they took it away, and were married next day
By the Turkey who lives on the hill.
They dined on mince, and slices of quince,
Which they ate with a runcible spoon;
And hand in hand, on the edge of the sand,
They danced by the light of the moon,
 The moon,
 The moon,
They danced by the light of the moon.

EDWARD LEAR (1812–1888)

1

2
Thomas Hardy born, 1840

3

4

5

6

7

NOTES

8

9

10

11

12

13

14

CAT ACTS

A black cat turning up in a theatre on a first night is a lucky omen for the opening of a show. Perhaps this is one of the reasons that many theatres have a house cat who is pampered by passing stars, in the hope he might turn up at the right time.

Some cats seem to simply love being in the spotlight; others prefer to stay in the wings, as well-loved mousers behind the scenes. T.S. Eliot insisted on allowing his cat Asparagus (Gus to the inner circle) to act as stage door minder during performances of Eliot's plays.

At the Adelphi theatre in London a couple of sibling cats called Plug and Socket were famous for marching through the stalls during play rehearsals, encouraging the actors. However, they never liked it when the show had started and would disappear once the public were privy to the performances that had until then been exclusively for their benefit.

Wonderland
ADELAIDE CLAXTON (*fl.1859–1879*)

*Gemini cats
are natural dramatists.*

15

16

17

18

19

20

21

NOTES

JUNE

Robbie, the CORNISH REX, sits up intently. Is there going to be a storm?

WARNING WAYS

Cats are well known for their ability to foretell all kinds of natural phenomena, such as the oncoming of electrical storms. They appear to be able to tell when a volcano is about to erupt or an earthquake about to happen. A cat will indicate this by showing extreme anxiety. In the case of an earthquake there are stories of cats rushing to get away from buildings which have later collapsed like cards. There are even stories of mother cats rushing to move their kittens out of buildings and to safety before any humans have been aware of what is about to happen.

If a cat washes over its ears it's sure to rain.
TRADITIONAL PROVERB

If a cat with it's back to the fire does sit This means storms and frost will shortly hit.

GEMINIS (MAY 22 –JUNE 22)

Charming, clever, curious and agile themselves, they are almost honorary cats, so doubly appreciate the cat's resourcefulness, curiosity and slippery agility. Cats sharing a restless Gemini home must be sure to arrange a back-up food supply; Geminis are often out having too good a time to bother about tiresome feeding routines.

22

23

24

25

26

27

28

NOTES

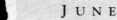

MY CAT JEOFFREY

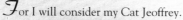

For I will consider my Cat Jeoffrey.

For he is the servant of the Living God, duly and daily serving him.

For at the First glance of the glory of God in the East he worships in his way.

For is this done by wreathing his body seven times round with elegant quickness.

For then he leaps up to catch the musk, which is the blessing of God upon his prayer.

For he rolls upon prank to work it in.

For having done duty and received blessing he begins to consider himself.

For this he performs in ten degrees.

For first he looks upon his fore-paws to see if they are clean.

For secondly he kicks up behind to clear away there.

For thirdly he works it upon stretch with the fore-paws extended.

For fourthly he sharpens his paws by wood.

For fifthly he washes himself.

For sixthly he rolls upon wash.

For seventhly he fleas himself, that he may not be interrupted upon the beat.

For eighthly he rubs himself against the post.

For ninthly he looks up for his instructions.

For tenthly he goes in quest of food.

For having consider'd God and himself he will consider his neighbour.

For if he meets another cat he will kiss her in kindness.

For when he takes his prey he plays with it to give it a chance.

For one mouse in seven escapes by his dallying.

For when his day's work is done his business more properly begins.

For he keeps the Lord's watch in the night against the adversary.

For he counteracts the powers of darkness by his electrical skin and glaring eyes.

For he counteracts the Devil, who is death, by brisking about the life.

For in his morning orisons he loves the sun and the sun loves him.

For he is of the tribe of Tiger.

For the Cherub Cat is a term of the Angel Tiger.

For he has the subtlety and hissing of a serpent, which in goodness he suppresses.

For he will not do destruction, if he is well fed, neither will he spit without provocation.

For he purrs in thankfulness, when God tells him he's a good Cat.

For he is an instrument for the children to learn benevolence upon.

For every house is incomplete without him and a blessing is lacking in spirit.

For the Lord commanded Moses concerning the cats at the departure of the Children of Israel from Egypt.

For every family had one cat at least in the bag.

For the English Cats are the best in Europe.

For he is the cleanest in the use of his fore-paws of any quadrupede.

For the dexterity of his defence is an instance of the love of God to him exceedingly.

For he is the quickest to mark of any creature.

For he is tenacious of his point.

For he is a mixture of gravity and waggery.

For he knows that God is his Saviour.

For there is nothing sweeter than his peace when at rest.

For there is nothing brisker than his life in motion.

For he is of the Lord's poor and so indeed is he called by benevolence perpetually - Poor Jeoffrey! poor Jeoffrey! the rat has bit thy throat.

For I bless the name of the Lord Jesus that Jeoffrey is better.

For the divine spirit comes about his body to sustain it in complete cat.

For his tongue is exceedingly pure so that it has in purity what it wants in music.

For he is docile and can learn certain things.

For he can set up with gravity which is patience upon approbation.

For he can fetch and carry, which is patience in employment.

For he can jump over a stick which is patience upon
proof positive.

For he can spraggle upon waggle at the word of command.

For he can jump an eminence into his master's bosom.

For he can catch the cork and toss it again.

For he is hated by the hypocrite and miser.

For the former is afraid of detection.

For the latter refuses the charge.

For he camels his back to bear the first notion of business.

For he is good to think on, if a man would express
himself neatly.

For he made a great figure in Egypt for his signal services.

For he killed the Ichneumon-rat very pernicious by land.

For his ears are so acute that they sting again.

For from this proceeds the passing quickness of his attention.

For by stroking of him I have found out electricity.

For I perceived God's light upon him both wax and fire.

For the Electrical fire is the spiritual substance, which God
sends from heaven to sustain the bodies both of man
and beast.

For God has blessed him in the variety of his movements.

For, tho he cannot fly, he is an excellent clamberer.

For his motions upon the face of the earth are more than any
other quadrupede.

For he can tread to all the measures upon the music.

For he can swim for life.

For he can creep.

JUBILATE AGNO (REJOICE IN THE LAMB)
A SONG FROM BEDLAM
CHRISTOPHER SMART (1722–1771)

29

30

NOTES

*Gemini cats are brisk and playful, always on the move;
this is the cat that will trek across counties in search of its humans.*

*God made the cat so that man might
have the pleasure of caressing the lion.*
FERNAND MERY

JULY

POLITICAL ANIMALS

TOM QUARTZ, the first cat to enter the White House under President Theodore Roosevelt's rule, was named after a fictional feline invented by the cat-loving author Mark Twain. John F. Kennedy's daughter Caroline introduced the next cat to the White House in the shape of Tom Kitten. President Bill Clinton also brought a bundle of fur in to the presidential residence, keeping going something of a tradition.

If a man could be crossed with a cat, it would improve the man but it would deteriorate the cat.

MARK TWAIN (1835–1910)

In Britain, Winston Churchill owned a cat during the Second World War that sat in on secret war meetings.

LET SLEEPING CATS LIE

*R*oosevelt later had a cat called Slippers, who tended to disappear for days and reappear at the wrong moment. One tale tells of how Slippers decided to splay out and snooze in the middle of a corridor carpet, just as a group of dignitaries were due to be led down to dinner along the very same corridor. Roosevelt gallantly led the state party in a swerve round the reclining cat, rather than upset the slumbers of his favourite feline.

MEWS FROM THE WHITE HOUSE

*T*om Quartz *is certainly the cunningest kitten I have ever seen. He is always playing pranks on Jack and I get very nervous lest Jack should grow too irritated. The other evening they were both in the library - Jack sleeping before the fire - Tom Quartz scampering about, an exceedingly playful creature - which is about what he is. . .*

Mr Cannon, an exceedingly solemn, elderly gentleman with chin whiskers, who certainly does not look to be of playful nature, came to call upon me. He is a great friend of mine, and we sat talking over what our policies for the session should be until about eleven o'clock and when he went away I accompanied him to the head of the stairs. He had gone about half-way down when Tom Quartz strolled by, his tail erect and very fluffy. He spied Mr Cannon going down the stairs, jumped to the conclusion that he was a playmate escaping, and raced after him, grasping him by the leg the way he does Archie and Quentin when they play hide and seek with him. . .

A LETTER TO HIS DAUGHTER, 6 JANUARY 1903
THEODORE ROOSEVELT

1

2

3

4

5
Jean Cocteau born, 1889

6

7

NOTES

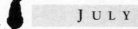

THE CUNNING CAT

*I*n the creation of animals, the cat came before its stronger sibling, the lion. When the newly-created lion arrived, it fell upon the cat to educate the clumsy creature. She devoted all her time to turning the lion into an agile animal. She showed him how to jump, how to pounce, how to wriggle undetected through the pampas grass. Finally, when the lion had learnt all the tricks, she took him on a hunt and showed him how to kill.

The lion, now filled with pride and stronger than all the animals around it, decided to test out all that it had learnt. It turned, unhappily upon its kindly teacher, the cat. Remembering every lesson she had taught him, the lion stalked her, then suddenly sprung, ready to kill.

The clever cat had foreseen the dangers involved in acting as an aunt to a creature that would one day test out its strength on her smaller, weaker frame. There was one lesson she did not teach the lion and that was how to climb a tree. As the lion sprung, she dashed for safety up the branches, for although smaller, she was wiser and older than the lion.

TRADITIONAL ARAB TALE

A typical Cancerian cat, *Pandora* watches cautiously from behind a protective tree.

CANCERIANS (JUNE 23 – JULY 23)

Imaginative, intuitive, cautious and contemplative, they appreciate the cat's intuition and ability to play a waiting game. Above all, home-loving, maternal Cancerians love to watch how well mother cats look after their offspring. The Cancerian home would be unthinkable without a cat or three – and, naturally, their kittens.

JULY

The word 'beasts' should properly be used about lions, leopards, tigers, wolves, foxes, dogs, monkeys and others which rage about with tooth and claw - with the exception of snakes. They are called beasts because of the violence with which they rage, and are known as 'wild' (*ferus*) because they are accustomed to freedom by nature and are governed (*ferantur*) by their own wishes. They wander hither and thither, fancy free, and they go wherever they want to go.

TWELFTH CENTURY BOOK OF BEASTS
TRANSLATED BY T. H. WHITE

July cats are modest and affectionate.

8

9

10

11

12

13

14

NOTES

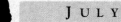

NURSERY RHYME CATS

I like little Pussy, her coat is so warm,
And if I don't hurt her she'll do me no harm;
So I'll not pull her tail, nor drive her away,
But Pussy and I very gently will play.

MOTHER GOOSE (C.1760)

*P*ussicat, wussicat, with
a white foot,
When is your wedding,
and I'll come to it.
The beer's to brew, the
bread's to bake,
Pussy cat, pussy cat, don't
be late.

TRADITIONAL

*P*ussy-cat Mole jumped over a coal,
And in her best petticoat burnt a great hole.
Poor pussy's weeping - she'll have no more milk
Until her best petticoat's mended with silk.

TRADITIONAL

15

16

17

18

19

20
Petrarch born, 1304

21

NOTES

 JULY

22

23

24

25

26

27
Alexandre Dumas born, 1824

28

NOTES

Pussy-cat sits by the fire;
How can she be fair?
In walks the little dog;
Says: 'Pussy, are you there?
How do you do, Mistress Pussy?
Mistress Pussy, how d'ye do?'
'I thank you kindly, little dog,
I fare as well as you!'

TRADITIONAL
NURSERY RHYME
MOTHER GOOSE
(C.1760)

JULY

Away from home, the cuddly house cat *Grimalkin*
scales a tree like a wild tiger.

*Cancerian cats have extra moon magic. Their moods change with
the moon's phases. They blend into the dark on moonless nights with
Hecate, witch goddess of the hidden moon; they hunt with bright
Diana, goddess of the new moon; and they produce their many litters
as homage to Silene, the goddess of the full moon, who looks after
lovers, lunatics and women in childbirth.*

SOULFUL STRAYS

Soulful strays are renowned for singling out new
homes and humans for themselves, where they
know they will be properly provided for with great love
and loyalty, often attaching themselves to equally stray
human souls. Sadly, some, as documented by the cat's
diary opposite, can never quite give up life on
the open road . . .

29

30

31

NOTES

Saturday:

I spent yesterday afternoon and evening at the home of a young child, whom I followed because she bore a paper of codfish which attracted me. The house where the child lives was exceedingly warm and pleasant, and I reclined in front of the glowing fire and made myself agreeable and attractive, considering meanwhile the advantages of such a home.

It has often occurred to me that sometime in my life I must have been owned. I can recall the feeling of caresses and the scent of soft garments worn by some gentle person who felt solicitude and affection for me. I think I can remember, though but dimly, the look of delicate white hands that cuddled me, and the warmth and sweetness of a breast to which I was pressed. How I ever became dissevered from all those comfortable conditions I do not know, but it was long ago, and has no part in my present life, for now I become restless in any close environment, and invariably after a short stay by some hearth of friendliness I feel the spell of the streets - a spell that draws me away from mere ease and plenty to thrill and mystery of a roving life. And so it was yesterday. Half slumbering on the little girl's lap after a delicious refreshment of custard and cold liver, I heard suddenly, or thought I heard, a voice that called me: and an old desire for vast lonely spaces, for the Desert of the Roofs, for silent cobbled streets, seized me. I thought of the vague gutters stretching away into solitude and night, and the old hungry haunting, the strong longing to go out and look for something, possessed me. I got down from the little girl's lap and went out of the door that led to the street.

THE DIARY OF A CAT
EDWINA STANTON BABCOCK

AUGUST

OLD CATS

HARDLY NOTICEABLE as you enter the room, the old cat is camouflaged in a favourite chair. The battered cushion is indented through years of experience to fit the feline curves exactly. ♪ Now slowly stretching one stiff paw, it is hard to imagine this slumbering shape once dancing in kittenhood. No longer jumping at the slightest sound, his slow breathing becalms the whole room as he dreams on and on and on. ♪ Humans tiptoe round him, like young students stealing fondly past an ageing professor, who has temporarily dozed off in the warm stilted air of some great seat of learning. An old cat is a creature who commands respect. ♪

AUGUST

1

2

3

4

5

6

7

NOTES

An old cat laps as much milk as a young.
ENGLISH PROVERB

TO MRS REYNOLDS' CAT

Cat! who hast pass'd thy grand climacteric,
How many mice and rats hast in thy days
Destroy'd? How many tit bits stolen? Gaze
With those bright languid segments
    green, and prick
Those velvet ears - but pr'ythee do
    not stick
Thy latent talons in me -
and upraise
Thy gentle mew - and tell me all
    thy frays,
Of fish and mice, and rats and
tender chick.
Nay, look not down, nor lick thy
dainty wrists -
For all thy wheezy asthma - and for all
Thy tail's tip is nick'd off - and though the fists
Of many a maid have given thee many a maul,
Still is that fur as soft, as when the lists
In youth thou enter'est on glass bottled wall.

JOHN KEATS (1795–1821)

Arise from sleep, old cat,
And with great yawns and stretchings
Amble out for love.

ISSA (1763–1827)

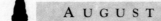

AUGUST

HOW DOGS, CATS AND MICE BECAME ENEMIES

In the olden days, when dogs, cats and mice lived together in perfect harmony, the dogs asked the cats to keep certain documents of great importance safely until they came back for them.

The cats looked at the pile of old papers, and they thought 'Why should we be bothered with these old scraps of paper? Let us ask the mice to take care of this queer treasure; it is just what they are fit for.' So they did, and the mice promised to keep an eye on the documents.

Meanwhile winter came, and a hard winter too. The poor little mice suffered from hunger and cold. In despair, they began to nibble at the old documents. The paper was not so bad, after all. So they gnawed and nibbled and ate the best parts, and tore the bad ones into tiny shreds, till there was not one whole piece.

At last, one day the dogs returned and wanted their documents back, so they went off to see the cats. But the cats said 'We thought it would be safer to give your documents to our friends the mice, so they keep them. Now we will go and fetch them for you.'

A pride of Leo kitties outstare an intrusive puppy.

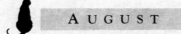

AUGUST

So off they went. But instead of the documents, they found only scraps of paper lying on the floor. The cats were furious. They vowed to kill every mouse they ever met in their way. But the dogs, when they heard the sad news, got angry too and began to chase the cats, and they have never stopped doing so ever since.

POLISH TRADITIONAL TALE

God made the cat so that man might have the pleasure of caressing the lion.
FERNAND MERY

8
Théophile Gautier born, 1897

9

10

11

12
Feast Day of St Francis of Assisi

13

14

NOTES

AUGUST

TO A CAT

*N*elly, methinks, 'twixt thee and me,
   There is a kind of sympathy:
And could we interchange our nature, -
   If I were cat, thou human creature, -
I should, like thee, be no great mouser
   And thou, like me, no great composer;
For, like thy plaintive mew, my muse,
   With villainous whine doth fate abuse,
Because it hath not made me sleek
   As golden down on Cupid's cheek;
And yet thou canst upon the rug lie,
   Stretch'd out like snail, or curl'd up snugly,
As if thou wert not lean or ugly;
   And I, who in poetic flights
Sometimes complain of sleepless nights,
   Regardless of the sun in heaven,
Am apt to dose till past eleven, -
   The world would just the same go round
If I were hang'd and thou wert drown'd;
   There is one difference, 'tis true,-
Thou dost not know it, and I do.

HARTLEY COLERIDGE (*1796–1849*)

LEOS (JULY 24–AUGUST 23)

Confident, courageous and charming, they are the big cats of the zodiac and so respect and protect all other cats as matter of course; they find it very easy to establish feline rapport. Cats living in a splendid Leo palace will be pampered and indulged. Leos love style and luxury and so long-haired Persians or big, impressive marmaladey toms are especially petted.

The Rivals
CHARLES BURTON BARBER (*1845–1894*)

AUGUST

15

16

17

18

19

20

21

NOTES

The cat makes himself the companion of your hours of solitude, melancholy and toil.
THÉOPHILE GAUTIER

CATTY CONVERSATIONALISTS

22

Pope Leo XII born, 1760

23

24

25

26

27

28

NOTES

They are much superior to human beings as companions. They do not quarrel or argue with you. They never talk about themselves, but listen to you while you talk about yourself, and keep up an appearance of being interested in the conversation. They never make stupid remarks. They never observe Miss Brown across the dinner-table, that they always understood she was very sweet on Mr Jones (who has just married Miss Robinson). They never mistake your wife's cousin for her husband, and fancy that you are the father-in-law. And they never ask a young author with fourteen tragedies, sixteen comedies, seven farces, and a couple of burlesques in his desk, why he doesn't write a play.

They never say unkind things. They never tell us of our faults, 'merely for our own good'. They do not, at inconvenient moments, mildly remind us of our past follies and mistakes. They do not say, 'Oh yes, a lot of use you are, if you are ever really wanted' - sarcastic like. They never inform us, like our in-amoratas sometimes do, that we are not nearly so nice as we used to be. We are always the same to them.

JEROME K. JEROME (1859–1927)

AUGUST

*Only those who have taken the trouble to cultivate
and study the cat can realise what an extraordinarily
intelligent and responsive creature he is.*
MICHAEL JOSEPH

29

30

31

NOTES

What is *Red*, the miniature lion, trying to say,
as he gazes into your eyes?

*Leo cats are the monarchs of the feline world; they
know that inside they are lions, proud and dignified.*

SEPTEMBER

Cat And Mouse

SHE IS CALLED MOUSER because she is fatal to mice. The vulgar call her CATU because she catches things (*a captura*) while others say that it is because she lies in wait (*captat*) i.e. because she 'watches'. So acutely does she glare that her eye penetrates the shades of darkness with a gleam of light. Hence from the Greek comes catus, i.e. 'acute'. ♪

A TWELFTH CENTURY BOOK OF BEASTS
TRANSLATED BY T. H. WHITE

Ever alert,
Jacob keeps
watch; Virgo cats
are excellent mousers.

VIRGOANS (AUGUST 23 –SEPTEMBER 23)
*Modest, meticulous and methodical, they appreciate
cats' neatness of body and fastidious cleaning routines.
Cats living within the orderly domain of a Virgo household
will be excellently looked after; but hardworking Virgo will
expect the cat to earn its keep as a mouser.*

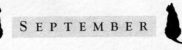

C was for Papa's gray Cat,
Who caught a squeaky Mouse;
She pulled him by his twirly tail
All about the house.

EDWARD LEAR (1812–1888)

L at take a cat and fostre hym wel with milk
And tendre flessch and make his couche of silk,
And lat hym seen a mouse go by the wal,
Anon he weyvith milk and flessch and al,
And every deyntee that is in that hous,
Suich appetit he hath to ete a mous.

GEOFFREY CHAUCER (1345–1400)

The cat, with eyne
of burning coal,
Now crouches fore
the mouse's hole.
WILLIAM SHAKESPEARE

1

2

3

4

5

6

7

NOTES

[499] Sept 7.
HAD SUPPER AT SUES. STARTED A COLD
NOT BAD. SARA KEPT BACK ESCORT
10 CHILDREN

THE CHESHIRE CAT

S he was a little startled by seeing the Cheshire Cat
sitting on a bough of a tree a few yards off.

The Cat only grinned when it saw Alice. It looked
good-natured, she thought: still it had very long claws and
a great many teeth, so she felt that it ought to be treated
with respect.

'Cheshire Puss,' she began, rather timidly, as she did
not at all know whether it would like the name: however,
it only grinned a little wider. 'Come, it's pleased so far,'
thought Alice, and she went on. 'Would you tell me,
please, which way I ought to go from here?'

'That depends a good deal on where you want to get
to,' said the Cat.

'I don't much care where - ' said Alice.

'Then it doesn't matter which way you go,' said
the Cat.

' - so long as I get somewhere,' Alice added as an
explanation.

'Oh, you're sure to do that,' said the Cat, 'if you only
walk long enough.'

*One explanation for the expression
'grinning like a Cheshire cat' was that in the
county of Cheshire, cheese was once sold moulded
in to the shape of a grinning cat.*

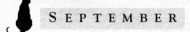
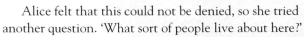

Alice felt that this could not be denied, so she tried another question. 'What sort of people live about here?'

'In that direction,' the Cat said, waving its right paw round, 'lives a Hatter: and in that direction,' waving the other paw, 'lives a March hare. Visit either you like: they're both mad.'

'But I don't want to go among mad people,' Alice remarked.

'Oh, you can't help that,' said the Cat: 'we're all mad here. I'm mad. You're mad.'

'How do you know I'm mad?' said Alice.

'You must be,' said the Cat, 'or you wouldn't have come here.'

Alice didn't think that proved it at all; however, she went on: 'And how do you know that you're mad?'

'To begin with,' said the Cat, 'a dog's not mad. You grant that?'

'I suppose so,' said Alice.

'Well then,' the Cat went on ' you see a dog growls when it's angry, and wags its tail when it's pleased. Now I growl when I'm pleased, and wag my tail when I'm angry. Therefore I'm mad.'

'I call it purring, not growling,' said Alice.

ALICE'S ADVENTURES IN WONDERLAND
LEWIS CARROLL *(1832–1898)*

8

9
Cardinal Richelieu born, 1585

10

11

12

13

14

NOTES

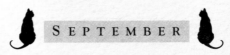

15

16

17

18
Dr Samuel Johnson born, 1709

19

20
Stevie Smith born, 1902

21

NOTES

VENUS AND THE CAT

A cat fell in love with the most handsome man she had every seen. After a while, the cat could bear it no longer. She entreated the Goddess Venus to change her form, so that the man might love her as a human being. Venus agreed to this unusual request and the cat became a gracious, beautiful lady, with exquisite green eyes.

The man fell in love with the lovely woman and begged her to become his bride. She agreed and they married at once. On the wedding night, they lay outstretched on their bed, when Venus set a little test for the cat lady. She wanted to see if the cat had altered her habits to suit her new shape, so Venus set down a mouse in the middle of the room.

The cat, forgetting altogether that she was a lady, leapt off the bed and to the horror of her lover began to pursue the mouse, with the intention of eating it.

Venus was very disappointed at this behaviour and returned the lady to her feline shape, saying that nature never exceeds nurture.

AESOP'S FABLES

22

23

24

25

26
T.S. Eliot born, 1888

27

28

Princess, small, neat and
self-possessed, is a typical
Virgo cat.

N O T E S

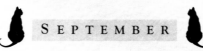 

DEAR CREATURE

The Cat

Dear creature by the fire a-purr,
  Strange idol eminently bland,
Miraculous puss! As o'er your fur
  I trail a neglible hand,

And gaze into your gazing eyes,
  And wonder in a demi-dream
What mystery it is that lies
  Behind those slits that glare and gleam,

An exquisite enchantment falls
  About the portals of my sense;
Meandering through enormous halls
  I breathe luxurious frankincense,

An ampler air, a warmer June
  Enfold me, and my wondering eye
Salutes a more imperial moon
  Throned in a more resplendent sky

Than ever knew this northern shore.
  O, strange! For you are with me too,
And I who am a cat once more
  Follow the woman that was you.

With tail erect and pompous march,
  The proudest puss that ever trod,
Through many a grove, 'neath many an arch,
  Impenetrable as a god,

Down many an alabaster flight
  Of broad and cedar-shaded stairs,
While over us the elaborate night
  Mysteriously gleams and glares!

LYTTON STRACHEY (1880 - 1932)

Cats seem to go on the principle
that it never does any harm to ask for
what you want.
JOSEPH WOOD KRUTCH

Pristine white socks and whiskers show
that *King* is a real Virgo puss.

29

30

NOTES

A Virgo cat is neat, scrupulous and self-possessed, the kind
of cat that tucks her tail tidily around her feet and is never
caught with her whiskers covered in cream.

OCTOBER

HOUSE CATS

A HOUSE BECOMES a home when it has a cat or two on the mat. Whether the resident puss is indoors or out, it has an ability to breathe an ubiquitously feline feel all around the house. Returning at the end of a busy day, nothing says 'home' quite so well as a greeting from a contented house cat.

The cat is the only non-gregarious domestic animal. It is retained by its extraordinary adhesion to the comforts of the house in which it is reared.
FRANCIS GALTON

I love cats because I love my home, and little by little they become its visible soul.

JEAN COCTEAU (1889–1963)

THE CAT OF THE HOUSE

*O*ver the hearth with my 'minishing eyes I muse
Until after
The last coal dies.
Every tunnel of the mouse,
Every channel of the cricket,
I have smelt.
I have felt
The secret shifting of the mouldered rafter,
And heard
Every bird in the thicket.
I see
You
Nightingale up in your tree!
I, born of a race of strange things,
Of deserts, great temples, great kings,
In the hot sands where the nightingale never sings!

FORD MADOX FORD *(1873–1939)*

A CAT

A cat I keep, that plays about
my House,
Grown fat with eating many a
miching Mouse.

ROBERT HERRICK *(1591–1674)*

A home without a cat, and a well-fed,
well-petted and properly revered cat, may be a perfect
home, perhaps, but how can it prove its title?

MARK TWAIN *(1835–1910)*

1

2

3

4

5

6

7

NOTES

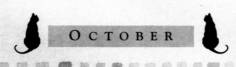

THE RAT CATCHER
AND THE CATS

The rats by night such mischief did,
Betty was ev'ry morning chid.
They undermined whole sides of bacon,
Her cheese was sapp'd, her tarts were taken.
Her pasties, fenced with thickest paste,
Were all demolish'd and laid waste,
She cursed the Cat for want of duty,
Who left her foes a constant booty.
An engineer of noted skill,
Engaged to stop the growing ill.
From room to room he now surveys
Their haunts, their works, their secret ways;
Finds where they 'scape an ambuscade,
And whence the nightly sally's made,
An envious Cat from place to place,
Unseen, attends his silent pace.
She saw that if his trade went on,
The purring race must be undone;
So, secretly removes his baits,
And ev'ry stratagem defeats.
Again he sets the poison'd toils.
And Puss again the labour foils.
What foe (to frustrate my designs)
My schemes thus nightly countermines?
Incensed, he cries, this very hour
The wretch shall bleed beneath my power.
So said, a pond'rous trap he brought,

And in the fact poor Puss was caught.
Smuggler, says he, thou shalt be made
A victim to our loss of trade.
The captive Cat, with piteous mews,
For pardon, life, and freedom sues.
A sister of the science spare;
One int'rest is our common care.
What insolence! the man replied;
Shall Cats with us the game divide?
Were all your interloping band
Extinquish'd, or expell'd the land,
We Rat-catchers might raise our fees,
Sole guardians of a nation's cheese!
A Cat, who saw the lifted knife,
Thus spoke, and saved her sister's life:
In ev'ry age and clime we see,
Two of a trade can ne'er agree.
Each hates his neighbour for encroaching;
'Squire stigmatizes 'squire for poaching;
Beauties with beauties are in arms,
And scandal pelts each other's charms;
Kings, too, their neighbour kings dethrone,
In hope to make the world their own.
But let us limit our desires,
Not war like beauties, kings, and 'squires!
For though we both one prey pursue,
There's game enough for us and you.

JOHN GAY (1685–1732)

 8

 9

 10

 11

 12

 13

 14

 NOTES

RATTY CATS

*C*ats have long been used as superior quality rat catchers. It was once a custom in Britain to build a cat and a rat together into the structure of a house. The cat would be placed in a predatory position over the rat and the home builders believed this would guard the house against an infestation of rats, although a living cat would probably have been a better bet.

When the cat is gone, out come the rats to stretch themselves.
CHINESE PROVERB

 OCTOBER

LIBRANS (SEPTEMBER 24 – OCTOBER 23)

*Charming, refined, graceful and genteel themselves, they
love beauty in all things and appreciate the harmonious
felicity of cats – as well as the fearful symmetry of tigers.
As subjects of Venus, Librans also respect the cat's
amorous imperative. Cats in the elegant Libra home must
be well-mannered and a class act; a beautiful long-legged
Burmese, perhaps, affectionate and yet aristocratic.*

15

16

17

18

19

James Leigh Hunt born, 1784

20

21

*Libra cats are handsome,
passionate lovers.*

NOTES

AN APPEAL TO CATS
IN THE BUSINESS OF LOVE

Ye cats that at midnight spit love at each other,
Who best feel the pangs of a passionate lover,
I appeal to your scratches and your tattered fur,
If the business of love be no more than to purr.
Old Lady Grimalkin with her gooseberry eyes,
Knew something when a kitten, for why she was wise;
You find by experience, the love-fit's soon o'er,
Puss! Puss! lasts not long, but turns to cat-whore!
Men ride for many miles,
Cats tread many tiles,
Both hazard their necks in the fray;
Only Cats, when they fall
From a house or a wall,
Keep their feet, mount their tails,
   and away!

THOMAS FLATMAN (*1635–1688*)

22

23

24

25

26

27
Theodore Roosevelt born, 1858

28

NOTES

CATS CAUGHT IN TROUBLE

Occasionally, puss will cause chaos by doing something that simply isn't cricket. In the case of the seventeenth-century poet Thomas Master, the sin in question was a little chomping and chewing indulged in by his cat, ruining his precious lute strings.

ON LUTESTRINGS CATT- EATEN

Are these the strings that poets feigne
    Have clear'd the Ayre, and calm'd the mayne?
Charm'd wolves, and from the mountaine creasts
    Made forests dance with all their beasts?
Could these neglected shreads you see
    Inspire a Lute of Ivorie
And make it speake? Oh! think then what
    Hath beene committed by my catt,
Who, in the silence of this night
    Hath gnawne these cords, and marr'd them quite;
Leaving such reliques as may be
    For fretts, not for my lute, but me.
Pusse, I will curse thee; may'st thou dwell
    With some dry Hermit in a cell
Where ratt neere peep'd, where mouse neere fedd,
    And flyes goes supperless to bedd;
Or with some close-par'd Brother, where
    Thou'lt fast each Saboath in the yeare;
Or else, prophane, be hang'd on Munday,
    For butchering a mouse on Sunday;
Or May'st thou tumble from some tower,
    And misse to light upon all fower,
Taking a fall that may untie
    Eight of nine lives, and let them flye;

Or may the midnight embers sindge
    Thy daintie coate, or Jane beswinge
Thy hide, when she shall take thee biting
    Her cheese clouts, or her house beshiting.
What, was there neere a ratt nor mouse,
    Nor Buttery ope? nought in the house
But harmeless Lutestrings could suffice
    Thy paunch, and draw thy glaring eyes?
Did not thy conscious stomach finde
    Nature prophan'd that kind with kind
Should stanch his hunger? thinke on that,
    Thou caniball, and Cyclops catt.
For know, thou wretch, that every string
    Is a catt-gutt, which art doth spinne
Into a thread; and how suppose
    Dunstan, that snuff'd the divell's nose,
Should bid these strings revive, as once
    He did the calfe, from naked bones;
Or I, to plague thee for thy sinne,
    Should draw a circle, and beginne
To conjure, for I am, look to't,
    An Oxford scholler, and can doo't.

    Then with three setts of
mapps and mowes,
    Seaven of odd words, and
motley showes,
A thousand tricks, that may
be taken
    From Faustus, Lambe or
Fryar Bacon:
I should beginne to call
my strings
    My catlings, and my
mynikins;
And they recalled, straight
should fall

To mew, to purr, to catterwaule
From puss's belly. Sure as death,
   Pusse should be an Engastranith;
Pusse should be sent for to the king
   For a strange bird, or some rare thing.
Pusse should be sought to farre and neere,
   As she some cunning woman were.
Pusse should be carried up and downe,
   From shire to shire, from Towne to Towne,
Like to the camell, Leane as Hagg,
   The Elephant, or Apish negg,
For a strange sight; pusse should be sung
   In Lousy Ballads, midst the Throng
At markets, with as good a grace
   As Agincourt, or Chevey-chase.
The Troy-sprung Brittan would forgoe
   His pedigree he chaunteth soe,
And singe that Merlin - long deceast -
   Returned is in a nyne-liv'd beast.
Thus pusse, thou seest what might betyde thee;
   But I forbeare to hurt or chide thee;
For may be pusse was melancholy
   And so to make her blythe and jolly,
Finding these strings, shee'ld have a fitt
   Of mirth; nay, pusse, if that were it,
Thus I revenge mee, that as thou
   Hast played on them, I've plaid on you;
And as thy touch was nothing fine,
   Soe I've but scratched these notes of mine.

THOMAS MASTER (1603–1643)

29

30

31

NOTES

*Libra cats are accomplished flirts; however naughty they
have been, they will soon charm their besotted owners into
forgiveness with a flick of their beautiful tails.*

November

A Communicative Cat

THE INTELLIGENCE OF CALVIN was something phenomenal, in his rank of life. He established a method of communicating his wants, and even some of his sentiments; and he could help himself in many things. There was a furnace register in a retired room, where he used to go when he wished to be alone, that he always opened when he desired more heat; but never shut it, any more than he shut the door after himself . . . 🐈 I hesitate a little to speak of his capacity for friendship and the affectionateness of his nature, for I know from his own reserve that he would not care to have it much talked about. We understood each other perfectly, but we never made any fuss about it; when I spoke his name and snapped my fingers, he came to me; when I returned home at night, he was pretty sure to be waiting for me near the gate, and would rise and saunter along the walk, as if his being there was purely accidental - so shy was he commonly of showing feeling. 🐈

MY SUMMER IN A GARDEN
CHARLES DUDLEY WARNER (1829–1900)

NOVEMBER

1

2

3

4

5

6

7
Feast Day of St Ambrose, patron saint of domestic animals

NOTES

Suki, a knowing Scorpio, communicates her feelings
with meaningful looks from her glowing eyes.

*N*ot only do feline friends communicate their own needs famously; they also have an uncanny ability to sense our moods without words. Somehow, a favourite cat will know where it is needed and settle comfortingly on the lap of an unhappy human. There it will stay until the constant sound of purrs pushes away even the most troublesome thoughts from the human mind.

GAMES AND RECREATIONS INCLUDING FIRESIDE READING, LETTER WRITING AND SMALL HOUSEHOLD REPAIRS

Bonny and *Clyde* are ready for a nap after playing with their ball.

The above categories don't refer to yours but to theirs, and they are not to be tolerated unless you, yourself, have something better to do. Any indulgence by your people in the above must be on sufferance and with your permission. You must establish firmly and quickly, once and for all, that they are not to participate in any of them if you happen to want attention. Under 'games' we consider any such pastimes as scrabble, dominoes, chess, checkers (and in the old days, mah-jongg), card games of any kind, ping-pong, badminton etc.

Every well-educated house cat ought to know when and how to break them up. For instance, there is no point in interfering with a scrabble game at the very beginning. They will only shoo you away, and if you persist, throw you out or shut you up in another room. Such procedure shows not only lack of instruction but failure to appreciate the psychology of people, which, in a house cat, is a far more serious defect. The proper method is to wait until the board is practically full with a most complicated arrangement of words. Then, jump up onto the board with the most sweetly saccharine 'Purrrrrrmaow' that you can muster, scatter the pieces in all directions, sit down, and commence to wash.

THE SILENT MIAOW
PAUL GALLICO (*1897–1976*)

THE PLAYFUL PUSS

We owe justice to men, and graciousness and benignity to other creatures that are capable of it; there is a certain commerce and mutual obligation betwixt them and us. . . When I play with my cat, who knows whether I do not make her more sport than she makes me? We mutually divert one another with our play. If I have my hour to begin or to refuse, she also has hers.

LORD MICHAEL MONTAIGNE
(*1533–1592*)

NOVEMBER

Scorpio kittens love to play power games.

8

9

10

11

12

13

14

NOTES

NOVEMBER

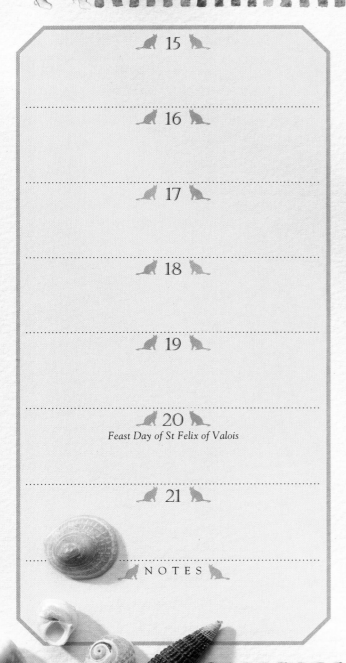

15

16

17

18

19

20
Feast Day of St Felix of Valois

21

NOTES

THE CAPTAIN'S CAT

*N*o ship in days gone by would set sail without a goodly cat or two amongst the crew to keep the mice from mincing through the grain stores.

THURSDAY, JULY 11TH, 1754
A most tragical incident fell out this day at sea. While the ship was under sail, but making as will appear no great way, a kitten, one of four of the feline inhabitants of the cabin, fell from the window into the water: an alarm was immediately given to the captain, who was then upon deck, and received it with the utmost concern and many bitter oaths. He immediately gave orders to the steersman in favour of the poor thing, as he called it; the sails were instantly slackened, and all hands, as the phrase is, employed to recover the poor animal. I was, I own, extremely surprised at all this: less indeed at the captain's extreme tenderness than at his conceiving any possibility of success; for if puss had had nine thousand instead of nine lives, I concluded they had been all lost. The boatswain, however, had more sanguine hopes, for having stripped himself of his jacket, breeches and shirt, he leaped boldly into the water, and to my great astonishment, in a few minutes returned to the ship, bearing the motionless animal in his mouth. Nor was this, I observed, a matter of such great difficulty as it appeared to my ignorance, and possibly may seem to that of my fresh-water reader. The kitten was now exposed to air and sun on the deck, where its life, of which it retained no symptoms, was despaired of by all. . . But as I have, perhaps, a little too wantonly endeavoured to raise the tender passions of my readers with this narrative, I should think myself unpardonable if I concluded it without giving them the satisfaction of hearing that the kitten at last recovered, to the great joy of the captain. . .

A VOYAGE TO LISBON
HENRY FIELDING (1707–1754)

NOVEMBER

22

23

24

25

26

27

28

NOTES

The ship's cat always brought sailors good luck. If the cat started the journey in a frisky mood, it was a good omen for the voyage ahead and meant good sailing. A cat that appeared annoyed at the journey's outset could indicate a difficult journey. Should a cat go overboard, a storm was sure to strike, so that sailors did their best to prevent puss ever falling into the sea.

However warm the saloon fire, however wet the deck, however rainy and stormy the weather, if the Captain is up on the deck, there the cat must be also.
ELINOR MORDAUNT

THE WANDERERS

Cat lovers everywhere will remember some time when their cat has disappeared and no amount of searching finds the beast. When the human heart is nearly broken by this, the cat will suddenly show up, never letting on where it has been, but making sure that its return will be celebrated with some special tit-bits.

Pussy-cat, Pussy-cat, where have you been?
I've been to London to see the Queen.
Pussy-cat, Pussy-cat, what did you there?
I frightened a mouse under the chair.

MOTHER GOOSE (C.1760)

THERE'S NO PLACE LIKE HOME

Two years ago the rightful owner of this cat discovered she was sharing its favours with three other households in the area. In all, four families were deluding themselves that it belonged to them. The cat apportioned its time with care and commendable fairness, slipping in and out daily for the odd snack or nap. When the extent of its infidelity was made public, a party was organised in the square in its honour, merely exemplifying, I'm afraid, our secret admiration for the successful fraud.

TOWN CATS
JOHN WEBB

Scorpio cats control
their own lives.

SCORPIOS (OCTOBER 24 – NOVEMBER 22)
Brooding and powerful, moody and
magnificent themselves, they appreciate the
cat's mesmerising stare and enigmatic power.
Only jet black cats with green eyes
need apply to lodge in a Scorpio home.

29

30
Winston Churchill born, 1874
Mark Twain born, 1835

NOTES

Scorpio cats are mysterious, magical and secretive; they are the cats who ride the broomsticks with the witches of the night.

W hence Hurlyburlybuss came was a mystery when you departed from the Land of Lakes, and a mystery it long remained. He appeared here, as Mango Gapac did in Peru and Quetzalcohuatl among the Aztecas, no one knew from whence. He made himself acquainted with all the philofelists of the family - attaching himself more particularly to Mrs Lovell, but he never attempted to enter the house, frequently disappeared for days, and once since my return for so long a time that he was actually believed to be dead and veritably lamented as such. The wonder was whither did he retire at such times - and to whom did he belong; for neither I in my daily walks, nor the children, nor any of the servants ever by any chance saw him anywhere except in our own domain.

LETTER TO HIS DAUGHTER (1824)
ROBERT SOUTHEY (1774–1843)

The elusive *Corker* returns from another mysterious sojourn into the November night.

DECEMBER

DELICIOUS DREAMS

CATS HAVE ALWAYS inspired jealousy. The amount of time they spend sleeping and the ease with which they doze off is often envied by their human owners. A sleeping cat can fill a room with an air of contentment. Yet of what do cats dream? A twitching paw and a strange, low growl emit from the slumbering bundle. Perhaps a dream of constant cream and fine fish. Or is poor puss pursued relentlessly by next door's dog?

Cats are rather delicate creatures and they are subject to a good many different ailments, but I never heard of one who suffered from insomnia.
JOSEPH
WOOD KRUTCH

DECEMBER

1

2

3

4

5

6

7

NOTES

LET SLEEPING CATS LIE

A poet's cat, sedate and grave,
As poet well could wish to have,
Was much addicted to enquire
For nooks to which she might retire,
And where, secure as mouse in chink,
She might repose, or sit and think.
I know not where she caught her trick –
Nature perhaps herself had cast her
In such a mould *philosophique*,
Or else she learn'd it of her master.
Sometimes ascending, debonair,
An apple tree or lofty pear,
Lodg'd with convenience in the fork,
She watched the gard'ner at his work;
Sometimes her ease and
    solace sought
In an old empty
    wat'ring pot,
There wanting
    nothing, save
    a fan,
To seem some
    nymph in her
    sedan,
Apparell'd in
    exactest sort,
And ready to be
    borne in court.

WILLIAM COWPER
(1731–1800)

8

9

10

11

12

13

14

NOTES

MUSICAL MOGGIES

The great nineteenth-century French feline lover, Théophile Gautier, had a cat called Madame Théophile. The cat loved to listen to singers as Gautier accompanied them on the piano. However, she disliked the female singers reaching a high note. In obvious distress at this sound, she would put her paw up to the singer's face and pat her on the mouth, as if to seal her lips. One theory is that the pitch was too similar to that of the sound of a distressed kitten for the maternal cat.

SAGITTARIANS
(NOVEMBER 23 – DECEMBER 22)
Independent, artistic, outgoing and free-spirited themselves, they admire the cat with the independent air, who loves and sings and leaps to her own rhythm. All cats are welcome at the hospitable Sagittarian home, as long as they can hold their own in the company of dogs.

DECEMBER

Will someone explain to me why the cat gets excited in a peculiar way, if you whistle to yourself very softly on a high note?...Perhaps in those remote and savage ages there lived some feline deities who to their faithful ones whistled with magic charm, but this is merely hypothesis, and the musical enchantment referred to is one of the mysteries of the cat's soul.

KAREL CAPEK

Ears strained for the music of distant drums, *Antony* and *Cleopatra* begin to dream of long, adventurous journeys.

15

16

17

18

19

20

21

NOTES

Wary Playmates

THE LOVER; WHOSE MISTRESS FEARED A MOUSE, DECLARETH THAT HE WOULD BECOME A CAT IF HE MIGHT HAVE HIS DESIRE

*I*f I might alter kind
   What think you, I would be?
Not Fish, nor Foule, nor Fle, nor Frog,
   Nor Squirrel on the Tree;
The Fish, the Hooke, the Foule
   The lymed Twig doth catch,
The Fle, the Finger, and the Frog
   The Bustard doth dispatch.

The squirrel thinking nought,
   That feately cracks the nut;
The greedie Goshawke wanting prey,
   In dread of Death doth put;
But scorning all these kindes,
   I would become a Cat,
To combat with the creeping Mouse,
   And scratch the screeking Rat.

I would be present, aye,
   And at my Ladie's call,
To gard her from the fearful Mouse,
   In Parlour and in Hall;
In Kitchen, for his Lyfe,
   He should not shew his hed;
The Pease in Poke should lie untoucht
   When shee were gone to Bed.

The mouse should stand in Feare,
   So should the sqeauking Rat;
All this would I doe if I were
   Converted to a Cat.

GEORGE TURBERVILLE *(1540–1610)*

DECEMBER

22

23

24

25

26

27

28

NOTES

For centuries, women have been praised and scorned in comparison with cats. While being kittenish is considered sweet, women are warned to 'keep their claws in' and not be 'catty' in their comments. However, for a woman to be described as feline is fairly complimentary – or so at least a cat would think.

Si Si rests after a long eventful outing.

DECEMBER

*I am not a friend, and I am not a servant.
I am The Cat Who walks By Himself, and I wish
to come into your cave.*
RUDYARD KIPLING

29

30
Rudyard Kipling born, 1865

31

NOTES

*Sagittarian cats are courageous explorers; these are the cats
that are found wandering happily miles from home or find
themselves stuck at the top of tall trees.*

MOURNING MOGGIES

The author Thomas Hardy adored cats and kept many of them throughout his life in rural Dorset, England. In the following poem, Hardy mourns the death of one of his cats but it appears that this was not a one-way feeling. In his last years, the writer had a beautiful blue Persian cat with amber eyes, called Cobby. When Hardy died, Cobby vanished forever, as if in mourning.

LAST WORDS
TO A DUMB FRIEND

Pet was never mourned as you,
    Purrer of the spotless hue,
Plumy tail, and wistful gaze
    While you humoured our queer ways,
Or outshrilled your morning call
    Up the stairs and through the hall -
Foot suspended in its fall -
    While, expectant, you would stand
Arched, to meet the stroking hand;
    Till your way you chose to wend
Yonder, to your tragic end.

Never another pet for me!
    Let your place all vacant be;
Better blankness day by day
    Than companion torn away.
Better bid his memory fade,
    Better blot each mark he made,
Selfishly escape distress
    By contrived forgetfulness,
Than preserve his prints to make
    Every morn and eve an ache.

From the chair whereon he sat
    Sweep his fur, nor wince thereat;
Rake his little pathways out
    Mid the bushes roundabout;
Smooth away his talons' mark
    From the claw-worn pine-tree bark,
Where he climbed as dusk embrowned,
    Waiting us who loitered round.

Strange it is this speechless thing,
    Subject to our mastering,
Subject for his life and food
    To our gift, and time, and mood;
Timid pensioners of us Powers,
    His existence ruled by ours,
Should - by crossing at a breath
    Into safe and shielded death,
By the merely taking hence
    Of his insignificance -
Loom as largened to the sense,
    Shape as part, above man's will,
Of the Imperturbable.

As a prisoner, flight debarred,
    Exercising in a yard,
Still retain I, troubled, shaken,
    Mean estate, by him forsaken;
And this home, which scarcely took
    Impress from his little look,
By his faring to the Dim
    Grows all eloquent of him.

Housemate, I can think you still
    Bounding to the window-sill,
Over which I vaguely see
    Your small mound beneath the tree,
Showing in the autumn shade
    That you moulder where you played.

THOMAS HARDY (1840–1928)

Paws For Proverbs

There are several hundred proverbs concerning cats which come from all around the world.

A CAT HAS NINE LIVES

One theory on the origin of this expression is that in ancient times nine was a lucky number because it is the trinity of trinities. As cats seem able to escape injury time and time again, this lucky number seemed suited to the cat. While in most countries the cat is said to have nine lives, in Arab and Turkish proverbs poor puss has a mere seven lucky lives and in Russia, is said to survive nine deaths.

He's as quiet
as a borrowed cat.
JAPAN

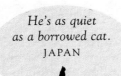

The cat who could not reach the meat roast declared
he would not eat it, to honour his father.
KURDISTAN

The man who
loves cats will
love his wife.
RUSSIA

My soul feels as
disturbed as if a cat were
treading on my heart.
CHINA

If stretching made
money, all cats would
be wealthy.
GHANA

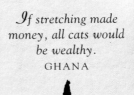

The cat wonders
at its own tail.
SPAIN

The cat is
a holy creature
until the milk
arrives.
INDIA

When the cat's
away, the mice will play.
ENGLAND

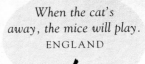

After a time,
even the dog
begins to
compromise with
the cat.
HUNGARY

A kind welcome
is beloved by a cat.
RUSSIA

When the cat winketh
Little kens the mouse
What the cat thinketh.
SCOTLAND

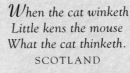

Whenever the cat
of the house is black
The lasses of lovers
will have no lack.
ENGLAND

Compiled, written and edited by Rhoda Nottridge
Additional material by Anna Clarkson
Designed by Peter Bridgewater
Photography by Guy Ryecart
Illustration by Lorraine Harrison
Page make-up by Chris Lanaway
Prop research and styling by Jane Lanaway
CLB 4305
© 1994 CLB Publishing, Godalming, Surrey, England

This 1995 edition published by Crescent Books, distributed by
Random House Value Publishing, Inc.
40 Engelhard Avenue, Avenel, New Jersey 07001
Random House
New York • Toronto • London • Sydney • Auckland
A CIP catalog record for this book is available from the Library
of Congress

Printed and bound in Singapore
ISBN 0-517-12138-7

9 8 7 6 5 4 3 2 1

🐾 BIBLIOGRAPHY 🐾

CAT'S COMPANY by Michael Joseph (Geoffrey Bles) CATWATCHING by Desmond Morris (Jonathan Cape)
IN PRAISE OF CATS by Dorothy Foster (Harrap) THE BOOK OF CATS by George Macbeth and Martin Booth
(Bloodaxe) THE CAT'S WHISKERS by Beryl Reid (Ebury Press) THE POETRY OF CATS
by Samuel Carr (Batsford) THE TRIUMPHANT CAT by Marmaduke Skidmore
(Robinson Publishing) TO MAKE A CAT LAUGH by E. E. Ralphs (Shearwater Press)

The publishers gratefully acknowledge permission to reproduce extracts from the
following material:

TOWN CATS by John Webb (Michael Joseph, 1980) by permission Michael
Joseph Ltd. THE SILENT MIAOW by Paul Gallico (Michael Joseph),
Copyright © 1964 by Paul W. Gallico and Suzanne Szasz. Copyright © 1964
Mathemata Anstalt.

Every effort has been made to trace all copyright holders. The editor and
publishers sincerely apologise for any inadvertent errors or omissions and
will be happy to correct them in any future edition.

🐾 ACKNOWLEDGEMENTS 🐾

Special thanks are given to the following, for their
kind and generous help in supplying photographic props.
Cat props: THE CAT SHOP, BRIGHTON *Front cover,* 1, 2, 3, 4, 5,
6, 7, 8, 10, 12, 15, 17, 19, 25, 27, 29, 31, 32, 40, 42, 43, 46, 52,
55, 58, 61, 62, 65, 67, 71, 72, 73, 75, 77, 79, 80, 81, 83, 87,
88, 95, 96, 100, 101, 106, 107; PATRICIA CROUCH *Front
cover;* PEGGY CLARKSON 104; LYANA LANAWAY 1, 2, 3,
4, 5, 6, 21, 23, 34, 36, 38, 44, 48, 50, 66, 68, 69, 78,
82, 91, 99, 103. *Lace:* CHRISTINE MARR 13, 36,
43, 48, 49, 52, 73, 96, 99; P. PARRY 15, 16, 27.
Other props: ROSE HOPKINS 13, 28, 55, 63;
PETER HOPKINS 58, 91, 93, 76; ROSEMARY
LANAWAY 65; KAREN RYECART 32; *Picture
credits:* JEREMY SPALL - 8, 11, 14, 17, 20, 21,
22, 24, 29, 33, 38, 41, 46, 49, 53, 54, 57, 60, 64,
73, 74, 78, 79, 89, 91, 92, 93, 97, 101, 102, 103;
FINE ART PICTURE LIBRARY - 13, 53, 68, 70, 102.